T5-ARO-570

Writing and Research on the Computer

Editor
Irene Gardner

Editorial Project Manager
Paul Gardner

Editor-in-Chief
Sharon Coan, M.S. Ed.

Illustrator
Ben DeSoto

Art Coordinator
Denice Adorno

Imaging
Alfred Lau

Product Manager
Phil Garcia

Acknowledgements
Sixteen images contained in this book are copyright 1997, 1996 T/Maker Company, a wholly owned subsidiary of Broderbund Software, from their ClickArt 125,000 collection. (*www.broderbund.com*)

Some information published in this book was reproduced with the expressed written consent of Carolyn Hinshaw of The Learning Space Board. (*www.learningspace.org*)

Publishers
Rachelle Cracchiolo, M.S. Ed.
Mary Dupuy Smith, M.S. Ed.

Authors

Kathleen Schrock,
Jan Wahlers,
and Mary Watkins

Teacher Created Materials, Inc.
6421 Industry Way
Westminster, CA 92683
www.teachercreated.com
ISBN-1-57690-163-7
©2001 Teacher Created Materials, Inc.
Reprinted, 2004
Made in U.S.A.

Table of Contents

Table of Contents (cont.)

About the Authors

Kathleen Schrock is presently the technology coordinator of the Dennis-Yarmouth Regional School District in South Yarmouth, Massachusetts, where she has been both a library media specialist and in her current position for over ten years. Her duties require both maintenance of all the technology and networking in the district as well as technology curriculum integration planning and teacher training. She is well-known in the education field as the creator of *Kathy Schrock's Guide for Educators* (http://discoveryschool.com/schrockguide), a Web site started in June of 1995 to help fellow educators identify curriculum-related Web sites to enhance their units of study. Kathy partnered with Discovery Channel School in early 1999 to provide a well-rounded and robust site. She is the author of numerous articles and reviews in such publications as *Classroom Connect, Multimedia Schools, Technology Pathfinder for Teachers and Administrators,* and *Technology Connection.* Kathy is also the author of four books: *Evaluation of Internet Web Sites: An Educator's Guide, A Beginner's Handbook to School and Classroom Web Pages, Microsoft Publisher for Every Day of the School Year,* and *Inquiring Educators Want to Know: TeacherQuests for Today's Teachers.* Presenting nationally in the areas of information literacy, search strategies, copyright issues, and Web site evaluation, Kathy received her B.S. in elementary/special education from Rutgers College in 1979 and her M.L.S. from Rutgers Graduate School of Library and Information Studies in 1981.

Jan Wahlers has spent 16 years in public and private education. For the past 13 years, she has taught English, computer applications, and video production classes at both the high school and middle school levels. Her innovative programs have won many awards including Service Learning awards from the Indiana Pacers and an award from the governors of the Great Lakes states and GTE. Jan has written several articles and booklets and presents workshops on the local, state, and national levels in the areas of Service Learning, writing across the curriculum, the Information Retrieval Skills (IRS) research method, the innovative use of technology in the classroom, Cable in the Classroom, and creative classroom practices. She has received grants for her work with the gifted and talented programs, video and television production classes, Service Learning, and unique classroom projects. Jan is currently the English department chair and teaches English and video and television production classes.

Mary Watkins has spent 27 years in public education, 18 as an elementary librarian and nine years as a middle school information specialist. Her creative programs have won numerous local, state, and national awards. She is also the founder of the Indiana Ronald McDonald House Library and spent four years as the first co-director of the Ball Memorial Hospital Library of Life, Love, and Laughter. She has published numerous articles and has co-authored a book on educational technology, worked in the area of Service Learning, presented educational workshops for the cable industry, and taught secondary education courses at Ball State University in Muncie, Indiana. Her innovative programs have won many awards including Service Learning awards from the Indiana Pacers. She is a widely respected educator who is known for her infectious enthusiasm and her ability to help fellow teachers obtain grants, present workshops, apply for state and national awards, and become more innovative in the classroom.

Introduction

Writing and researching reports using the computer has changed dramatically in the last few years. Access to interactive CD-ROM's, the Internet, and other pieces of software for collection and storage of data has made the process more complex for both teachers and students. This book will offer the teacher tips, tricks, and proven methods to help teach research skills. It will also provide lessons for student use when formulating the research question, conducting the research, and evaluating the results. You will notice that some of the lessons in this book don't utilize a computer at all. Conducting research with a computer does not simply mean sitting down and using a computer for all tasks. The thinking process, the narrowing of topics, the practice with identification of keywords, and even Web site evaluation are often done before or after using a computer. The inclusion of a formalized research model in this publication also provides the educator with the information needed to effectively utilize research to support teaching across the curriculum.

The CD-ROM included with this book contains all of the handouts in Adobe Acrobat™ (PDF) format. If you do not have the free Adobe Acrobat reader, point your browser to http://adobe.com/ to find the version for your computer platform. There is a single Web page on the included CD-ROM that you can open in your browser, which will easily link you to all of the PDF files on the CD-ROM.

Also included on the CD-ROM are database templates to help students collect and arrange their data in a usable format. These templates will be found in DBF format for easy importing into *Microsoft Works™, AppleWorks™, Filemaker Pro™,* or *Microsoft Access™*.

Chapter 1: Introduction to Research

What is Research?

Research is the process, which includes an organized study of a subject. All research is documented, which means that the sources used are credited. It's fine to use someone else's ideas or words as long as credit is given. There is a difference between reports and research papers. Remember that students must prove something when writing a research paper. They must not simply "spit back" information found in books and other sources. In the past, students may have opened up an encyclopedia or a book and written down a great deal of information about a topic. These days, teachers and students realize that this type of reporting requires very little thinking. Writing a research paper or presenting a research project is different and requires a great deal of thinking!

The Purpose of Research

The purpose of research is to:
- allow the student to satisfy their curiosity and special interests in an area of study.
- help the student to make an organized search for, and presentation of, the information.
- allow the student to understand how a formal research study, research paper, or research presentation is organized and developed.
- allow the student to make use of the library, computer, and community resources to answer a question.
- allow the student to inquire in depth about a particular topic.

Parts of a Research Paper

The three essential parts of a research paper are:
1. Outline—an overview of the main topics and areas of the paper.
2. Essay—the actual body of the paper. It also includes the footnotes.
3. Works Cited—this area contains all the sources cited with footnotes in the paper.

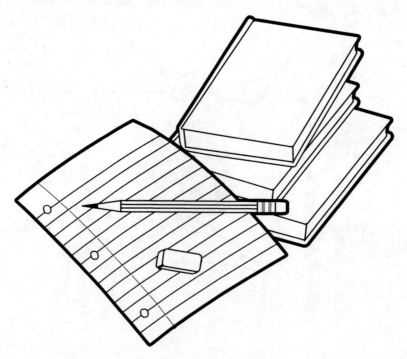

Chapter 1: Introduction to Research *(cont.)*

Steps in Writing a Research Paper

This book will take the students through the steps needed to write a research paper. The general overview of writing a research paper includes the following steps:

1. Select a general topic of interest.

2. Think about what knowledge you already have on this topic. Jot down some keywords that come to mind when thinking about this topic.

3. Look for general information about the topic. Encourage students to be realistic since they probably have a limited amount of time to complete this project, and they should be sure that enough information is available.

4. Narrow or focus the topic to meet the length of the paper or presentation.

5. Develop a thesis statement, which will guide further research and writing of the paper.

6. Write a beginning outline. This outline may have two to four subtopics that will be the main area of research to support the thesis statement.

7. Begin to gather information. Write down the important bibliographic information about the source, so a works cited page can be created later.

8. Write a more detailed outline of the research paper.

9. Write the first draft of the paper, including the footnotes when information from others is used.

10. Revise and write the final draft.

11. Create the works cited page by alphabetizing the sources in the method instructed by the teacher. Remember, there should be nothing listed on the works cited page that is not used in the paper.

Chapter 2: Choosing a Topic

Overview

One of the hardest things for a student to do is to narrow down a topic to research. With the huge amount of information available to search, it is very important that the initial research question be as specific as possible. If you are assigning the topics for the class, remember to be very precise with the subjects that are suggested as possible topics.

This chapter covers some of the pre-research skills necessary for successful identification of a topic. The first lesson, "What I Know," uses students' prior knowledge to complete a graphic organizer on a specific topic. By asking students to list what they know about a topic and what they think they know about a topic, it is easy to lead them into a conversation about what they might still want to know about the topic.

The next lesson, "Unlocking the Keywords," allows students to practice identifying keywords. Learning what constitutes a keyword in a paragraph is an important research skill that will be used when reading print or electronic sources, or formulating queries with online resources.

The "General Information" lesson presents the students with the background knowledge needed to conduct further research. Use of general purpose reference sources to allow identification of keywords and key topics will form the basis for further research on a specific topic.

Clarification and narrowing down of a research thesis statement is the subject of the "Fun and Games" lesson. Students are asked to come up with a Jeopardy-like question to a given answer. At the end of the lesson, students are asked to create a question that they would like to answer for their individual research projects.

The first use of the computer for this project by the students is incorporated into the lesson entitled "Roadmap for Research." By completing a graphic organizer template produced in *Inspiration*™, students will visually create their beginning search strategy. They should be encouraged to re-create, edit, and re-edit the strategy as they work towards their final research project.

I want to know if wrestling is a real sport. . .

Lesson Plan: What Do I Know? Think I Know? Want to Know?

For the Teacher

A useful method for generating topics and activating student prior knowledge is to first brainstorm topics with the entire class using the "What Do I Know? Think I Know? Want to Know?" worksheet on page 10.

Objectives

To activate student knowledge and introduce new concepts about a subject.

To help students identify topics for further research.

Materials

- Overhead projector and transparency of the "What Do I Know?" worksheet (page 10) OR
- Computer and projection device and the "What Do I Know" file from the CD-ROM

Procedures

With Overhead

1. Make a transparency of the sheet and complete this exercise on the overhead.

2. Fill in the first two columns as a group.

3. Duplicate the overhead onto paper and allow the students to individually fill in the "What I Want to Know" column. The completion of the sheet can be done individually or in small groups.

4. Conference with the students to talk about the topics they wish to choose from the last column.

With Computer and Projection Device

1. Use the Rich Text Format version found on the CD-ROM with *Microsoft Word*™, *Microsoft Works*™, *ClarisWorks*™, or *AppleWorks*™ to fill in the chart with the whole group.

2. Students can then add their third column directly on the computer and save a copy in their own folder on the computer.

Evaluation

Students will complete the worksheet and choose a topic for further research.

Name: _____ Date: _____

What Do I Know? Think I Know? Want to Know?

Topic: _____

As a group, brainstorm information about a topic. Come up with facts that you know and facts that you think you know. Then, in small groups or by yourself, fill in the column with the heading "What I Want to Know." From the information in this column, you will be meeting with your teacher to choose a topic for your report.

What I Know	What I Think I Know	What I Want to Know

Lesson Plan: Unlocking the Keywords

For the Teacher

One of the important skills in the research process is the ability to identify the keywords in a sentence or paragraph. By practicing with identification of keywords, students will find the process of searching for information much easier when they begin their formal research.

Objectives

Students will be able to identify keywords found in a sentence.

Students will generate related search terms that may be used to find the answer to the questions.

Materials

- "Unlocking the Keywords" worksheet (page 12) for each student
- Overhead projector and transparency of worksheet

Procedures

1. The teacher will explain that a keyword is often the topic word in a sentence.
2. Working with the overhead projector and the transparency, the teacher will complete the first few sentences with the students as a large group.
3. The keywords in each sentence will be underlined, and other related terms will be listed.
4. Each student will complete the worksheet individually and share his/her results with a small group.

Evaluation

Students will complete the worksheet and compare their results with others in the class.

Name: _____ Date: _____

Unlocking the Keywords

To begin to search for information, it is important to be able to identify the main words, called keywords, in a sentence.

Once the keywords are identified, it is easier to identify other words that may be used to look for information about a topic.

Underline the keywords in each sentence below, and list two or three other words dealing with the topics of the keywords.

1. There are many trading card games that students like to play.
   Other related words: _____

2. Motocross bicycles are very popular with students in fourth grade.
   Other related words: _____

3. One of the favorite playground games during recess is tag.
   Other related words: _____

4. Many students are reading the "Harry Potter" series of books.
   Other related words: _____

5. Yahooligans is a directory of Internet sites for students.
   Other related words: _____

6. The Internet is a worldwide network of computers that are all hooked together.
   Other related words: _____

Lesson Plan: General Information

For the Teacher

Once the general topic has been chosen, the students should be taken to the library to locate and read a few general articles about their topic. These articles can be those found in both hard copy and CD-ROM encyclopedias. Students should take notes on the "General Information" worksheet (page 14). Once the general information is collected, the students should have a clearer idea of the type of information they are looking for in relation to their topic.

Objectives

Students will identify key points dealing with their topic.

Students will conduct pre-research using note-taking strategies.

Students will peer evaluate work.

Materials

- "General Information" worksheet (page 14) for each student
- Hard copy encyclopedias or CD-ROM encyclopedias

Procedures

1. Each student uses an encyclopedia to identify key terms, topics, and related information about his/her research topic.

2. The students fill in the sheet to use for further research information.

3. In pairs, students discuss their findings and jot down any further thoughts.

Evaluation

Each student successfully completes the "General Information" worksheet.

Students are able to verbalize and generalize their findings to another student.

Name: _____ Date: _____

General Information

The General would like you to collect information about your topic. Using an encyclopedia, find information on your subject. As you are reading, write down any specific words or phrases that you think may be helpful. Also write down anything you want to learn more about. When you are done, discuss what you have written with a partner, and write down any other thoughts you might have.

Topic:_____

Words dealing with my topic:

Important phrases to remember:

Things I don't understand:

Things I thought about when talking with my partner:

The name and volume number of the encyclopedia I used:

_____ Volume number:_____

Lesson Plan: Fun and Games

For the Teacher

One of the hardest parts for students when conducting research is the ability to clarify what they are really looking for. With the general research complete, students should now be able to create their thesis statement or question. The clarification and narrowing down of a topic is a hard skill for students of any age. Practice with the samples provided in the lesson plan should allow the students to get a feel for what will be expected of them.

Objectives

Students will learn to narrow down the subject of a paragraph to one sentence.
Students will practice creating a question to go along with a paragraph of information.

Materials

- "Fun and Games" worksheet (page 16) for each student
- Projection device for large group work
- Completed "General Information" worksheet (page 14)

Procedures

1. The teacher will read the first paragraph on the page aloud. Students should be reminded of previous work that they have done in class with topic sentences. They should then be asked to write down the subject of the paragraph in one sentence.

2. Given an answer, students will be asked to create a "Jeopardy" type question to show that they understand what the main topic of the sentence might be. They will then need to create a question that is answered by the paragraph.

Evaluation

Students will be asked to write down a question for which they want to find the answer to in their research. They should consult their "General Information" worksheet to remind them of what they have already found.

Name: _____   Date: _____

Fun and Games

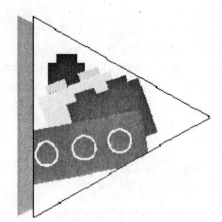

Blocks have always been a popular toy for children of all ages. Blocks were first made of wood. About one hundred years ago, they began to make them of plastic. Today, blocks may be found in almost every child's toy box.

The main topic of this paragraph is:

_____

_____

Games for children have changed over the years. In colonial times, children would use items that were available to make their own games. One such example was the use of a barrel stave and a stick to create a rolling hoop game in which children would race across the lawn to see who would come in first.

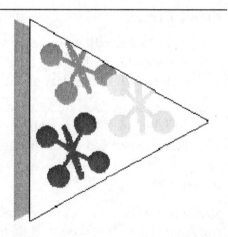

A question to which the above paragraph would supply the answer is:

_____

_____?

The question I would like to find the answer to for my research project is:

_____?

Lesson Plan: Roadmap for Research

For the Teacher

The use of an outline, or graphic organizer, is a good way for students to create the "roadmap" they will need to conduct their research. Using a program such as *Inspiration*™, the students can easily create their own outlines in a graphical format. For these grade levels, it would be best for you to create a template for students to use, and have them fill in the boxes. Students should be encouraged to edit this graphic organizer as they find out additional information or change the direction of their research. It is a good idea to have them save all versions, so they are able to reflect on the research process.

Objectives

Students will identify the key topics, keywords, and related materials they will be using to conduct their research.

Students will become familiar with the use of a computerized flowchart program.

Materials

- "Roadmap for Research" handouts (pages 18–19) for each student
- Computer with *Inspiration*™ software
- Large screen projection device

Procedures

1. The teacher will demonstrate the proper method for opening, closing, and saving an *Inspiration*™ file on the computer with the large group.

2. The teacher will open the template file and talk about the various pieces of information that need to be added. Students will have a printed copy of the template file.

3. A completed sample of a graphic organizer will be distributed to students so they can see the type of information that needs to be included.

Evaluation

Students will print out the first draft of their "Roadmap" templates so that they can bring it to the library media center and begin collecting information for their projects.

Name: _____ Date: _____

Roadmap for Research

This page shows the information that is included in the "Roadmap" template in the *Inspiration™* folder on the computer.

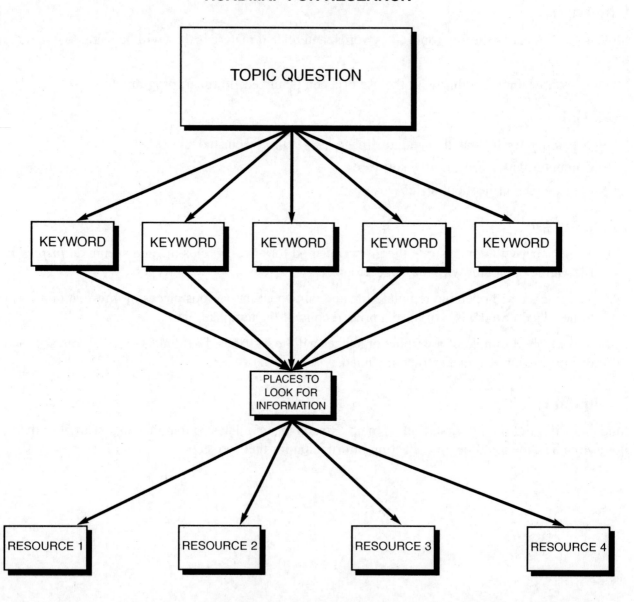

You will need to fill in each box with information about your research. Save the template to your folder, then print out the "Roadmap" to take to the library media center.

Name: _____ Date: _____

Roadmap for Research

Below is a sample of a completed "Roadmap for Research" template.

ROADMAP FOR RESEARCH

What has Bill Elliott done in NASCAR?

Bill Elliott	NASCAR	stockcar racing	Winston Cup	McDonald's Racing

PLACES TO LOOK FOR INFORMATION

Library card catalog	Sports section of newspaper	Internet	ESPN NASCAR show

Chapter 3: Documenting Information

Overview

This chapter contains lessons that teach the students the process and procedures for documenting the information that is going to be collected.

The "Menu for Success" lesson (page 21) demonstrates to the students the proper way to create bibliographic citations for the most common types of research materials. A handout with sample citations is included, and practice is provided via a worksheet, library media center, and classroom materials.

The next lesson, "Home (Data) Base," (page 25) targets the fact that the best time to incorporate the computer as a tool with the students is before beginning to actually collect information. This is the time when the database becomes the focus of instruction as a place to compile information as it is collected. This lesson allows the students to enter information into a database and retrieve requested information.

The "Database Entry Information Sheet" (page 28) includes a sample record form from a database. This form allows students to easily collect the data needed to create bibliographic citations for entry into the database.

Lesson Plan: Menu for Success

For the Teacher

The format for the bibliographic citations included here is simple and demonstrates to students the importance of being consistent. The practice in this lesson is based on pencil and paper. Later lessons take advantage of a database and an online bibliography maker.

Objectives

Students will learn the correct bibliographic format for citing various types of information.

Students will learn how to find the appropriate bibliographic information in the resource they are using.

Materials

- Various print sources—encyclopedia, atlas, almanac, non-fiction book, fiction book, newspaper, magazine
- Various electronic sources—CD-ROM encyclopedia, CD-ROM reference tool, Internet site printed out with headers and footers
- "Menu for Success" handouts (pages 22–23) and worksheet (page 24) for each student

Procedures

1. The teacher will explain the importance of giving credit to the author of the information that is being used for a report. This would be a good time to bring in the concept of copyright as defined as "the work of anyone that is published which is protected by law."

2. The teacher/library media specialist will demonstrate where the needed information for citing each source may be found. He/she should also emphasize that collection of this data is standardized.

3. Students will work in small groups or individually to create the bibliographic citations for the items that the teacher provides.

Evaluation

The students will complete the "Menu for Success" bibliographic citation worksheet successfully.

Name: _____ Date: _____

 **Menu for Success for Bibliographic Citations**

The process of collecting information about items that are used for your report is always the same. You will simply follow the menu of steps below to collect the information you will need to give credit to the author of the information. Punctuation is important!

••

For a book with one author:

Author, last name first.
Title of book. (underlined)
City of publication: Publisher, date of publication.

Example:
Simon, Seymour. <u>Hurricanes</u>. New York: McGraw-Hill, 1996.

••

For a book with two authors:

Authors, in order they are listed on the title page.
Title of book. (underlined)
City of publication: Publisher, date of publication.

Example:
Buffet, Jimmy and Tom Chapin. <u>Songs for Kids</u>. New York: Harper, 1999

••

For an encyclopedia article:

Author of article (if available).
"Title of article."
Title of encyclopedia. (in italics)
Volume number.
Date of edition,
Page number(s).

Example:
Smith, Mort. "Gemstones." *World Book Encyclopedia.* v.6. 1999, pp. 340–345.

••

Menu for Success (cont.)

For CD-ROM information:

Author (if available).
"Title of article."
Title of product (in italics).
Edition or version (if included).
CD-ROM.
City of publication: Publisher, date of publication.

Example:
Smith, John. "Franklin, Benjamin." *Microsoft Encarta*. 1999 ed. CD-ROM.
Redmond, WA: Microsoft Corporation, 1999.

Article in a magazine or newspaper:

Author (if available).
"Title of article."
Magazine or newspaper title (underlined). Date: page.

Example:
Schrock, Rockwell. "New Card Games for Kids." The New York Times.
22 December 1999: 34.

World Wide Web information:

Author (if known).
"Title of article."
Title of complete work (if known, underlined).
Date of visit.
<full URL> (in angle brackets).

Example:
Smith, Terry. "Exhibits at the Fair." Terry's 1904 Worlds Fair Page. 21 December
1999. <http://www.inlink.com/~terryl/exhibits.html/>.

Name: _____ Date: _____

Menu for Success

Using the reference materials your teacher has supplied, write the correct citation for each type. Refer to the examples on your "Menu for Success" handouts.

....

A book with one author:

_____

_____

A book with two authors:

_____

_____

An encyclopedia article:

_____

_____

A magazine or newspaper article:

_____

_____

A CD-ROM resource:

_____

_____

A Web site:

_____

_____

Lesson Plan: Home (Data) Base

For the Teacher

This lesson teaches students the use of a database for collecting data. This lesson will show students how this type of software can be used to collect data that can then be easily accessed, retrieved by various criteria, and used for different purposes.

The database on the CD-ROM is in a DBF format that may be imported into any standard database program. It is also included in *Microsoft Access*™ *97* and *2000* formats, *Filemaker Pro*™ format, *AppleWorks*™ format, and *Microsoft Works*™ format.

Objectives

Students will learn to open a database and enter information.

Students will learn to retrieve information in a database by different criteria.

Materials

- Computer and large screen projection device
- Access to a computer lab, if possible
- Completed "Menu for Success" worksheet (page 24)
- "Home (Data) Base Information Sheet" (page 26) for each student

Procedures

1. The teacher will demonstrate to students, in conjunction with a computer teacher if applicable, the appropriate way to open a database, enter information, move through the fields in the database, and search for information in a database. The use of a baseball metaphor will be used to describe the four basic steps in this process.

2. The teacher will then demonstrate the ways to search for information in a database to come up with matching records. This is specific to the piece of software being used as database software.

Evaluation

Students will successfully enter the bibliographic information from the "Menu for Success" worksheet (page 24) into the database on the computer.

Students will retrieve specifically requested information from the information in the database.

Name: _____ Date: _____

Home (Data) Base Information Sheet

The use of a database is an important tool for collection and use of data. There are four main steps to take advantage of the power of a database.

First Base

1. The first thing to learn is how to open a blank database and do a "Save As" to rename the file to your name. This way, you have your own database. When you have completed this task, move on to Second Base.

Second Base

2. The next thing to learn in a database is how to add a new record. Once you have opened a new record, added some information, and then opened another new record to add information, move on to Third Base.

Third Base

3. One thing to remember when using a database is to tab through the fields in a database to get to the field you want. Here, you may enter or change information. Once you have successfully tabbed through a record, go to Home Base.

Home Base

4. The most powerful feature of a database is the ability to search for a record by certain information. Search your database by a specific year of publication. How many sources did you use from that particular year?

Lesson Plan: Database Entry

For the Teacher

The students will be collecting their content and bibliographic information on the included database worksheets (or via an *AlphaSmart*™ or *Dreamwriter*™ if you have access to them) and then entering the information into their own database, either in the classroom or in the computer lab.

Objectives

Students will begin to compile information for their research reports.

Students will practice entering data into a database.

Materials

- "Database Entry Information Sheet" (page 28) for each student
- Access to a computer or computer lab

Procedures

1. Review the previous lessons on database entry, data retrieval, and the correct format of bibliographic citations. Students will then go to the library media center to begin collecting information for their research topic.

2. The classroom teacher and library media specialist will work together with the students to help them collect the bibliographic information needed for entry in to the database.

3. Once a student has collected five different resource pages, they will enter the data into the database.

Evaluation

Students will successfully gather bibliographic information and information for their reports and enter the collected data into a database.

Database Entry Information Sheet

Date	Name	Type of item	Author 1

Author 2

Title of article

Title of book_publication

Edition_version	CD ROM	Place of publication	State of publication

Publisher	Year of publication	Date of Web site visit

URL

Page number for articles

Information from resource

Notes to myself:

Chapter 4: Collecting Information

Overview

Before students are sent to the library media center or onto the Internet to collect information, it is important they learn about specific data collection strategies and are familiar with questions that should be asked when gathering information.

The first lesson, "Oodles of Outlines," helps the students understand the concept behind the three main types of outlines. They practice creating the three types of outlines after learning about each type.

For the Teacher

In order to make the data collection time as fruitful as possible, students should create a series of outlines before going to the library media center. They already have a basic knowledge of their topic from previous lessons and need to organize their thoughts and ideas before continuing.

There are three major types of outlines. All of them are based on the premise that information should be arranged hierarchically, although each one includes a different format of information.

- **Keyword outline**—the student uses only keywords at each level of the outline

- **Topic outline**—the student uses phrases at each level of the outline

- **Sentence outline**—the student uses complete sentences at each level of the outline

Each heading should correspond with a paragraph or part of the research project. The ideal outline has the opening sentence or topic of each paragraph as the highest level in each section.

Lesson Plan: Oodles of Outlines

Objective

Students will become familiar with the three major types of outlines.

Materials

- Copy of <u>The Little Red Lighthouse and the Great Gray Bridge</u> by Hildegarde H. Swift and Lynd Ward
- Children's picture book for each student
- Transparency of each type of outline type to share with students
- Sample outlines (pages 31–33) for each student

Procedures

1. The teacher will read <u>The Little Red Lighthouse and the Great Gray Bridge</u> aloud to the class.
2. The teacher will share the three versions of the outline of the book with the students.
3. The students will each read a children's picture book from the selected pile.
4. The students will create three versions of their outline of the book.
5. The outlines will be placed on top of the book, and the class will do a round-robin, reading each other's outlines and reading the book.
6. The students will then create one outline based on their thoughts for their project.

Evaluation

Each student will complete three outlines based on the subject of his/her picture book and one outline dealing with his/her project.

Sample Outlines for <u>The Little Red Lighthouse & the Great Gray Bridge</u>

Keyword Outline

   I. Lighthouse

      A. Red

      B. New York City

      C. Hudson River

  II. Lighthouse Keeper

      A. Daily

      B. Lights gas

 III. Bridge

      A. Gray

      B. Big

 IV. Storm

      A. Accident

      B No light

      C. Light on

Sample Outlines for <u>The Little Red Lighthouse & the Great Gray Bridge</u> *(cont.)*

Topic Outline

  I. Lighthouse on the shore

    A. Round and fat and red

    B. Near New York City

    C. In the Hudson River

  II. Had a lighthouse keeper

    A. Arrived daily

    B. Lit the gas tanks for light

 III. Bridge was built

    A. Gray and steel

    B. Bigger than lighthouse

 IV. Storm happened

    A. An accident occurred

    B Lighthouse not on

    C. Keeper finally arrives

    D. Lighthouse shone again

Sample Outlines for <u>The Little Red Lighthouse & the Great Gray Bridge</u> *(cont.)*

Sentence Outline

I. There was a lighthouse on the shore.

    A. The lighthouse was red and round.

    B. The lighthouse was on the Hudson River in New York City.

    C. The lighthouse kept the waters safe.

II. The lighthouse had a lighthouse keeper.

    A. The keeper came each day.

    B. The keeper lit the gas tanks that were used to produce the light.

III. A bridge began to be built over the lighthouse.

    A. The bridge was gray and made of steel.

    B. The bridge was much bigger than the lighthouse.

IV. A big rainstorm occurred.

    A. One of the ships on the river ran aground.

    B. The lighthouse did not have its light on.

    C. The lighthouse keeper finally arrived during the storm.

    D. The lighthouse shown its light to keep the boats and ships safe.

Lesson Plan: Questions to Myself

For the Teacher

A good researcher questions all information before using it. Some questions a researcher may ask include:

- How does this information change what I think I know about this topic?
- How does this information fit in with other information I have collected?
- Is this new information confusing?
- Is this new information different from other information I have collected?
- Does this information answer my thesis question?
- What do I still need to find out about my topic?
- Did I write down the bibliographic information about my topic?

Objectives

Students will understand the need to question the information they are finding and relate it to prior knowledge and current purpose.

Materials

- Three-paragraph non-fiction passage
- "Questions to Myself" worksheet (page 35)
- "Questions to Myself Checklist" (page 36)

Procedures

1. The teacher will share a three-paragraph passage from a social studies book, Web page, or encyclopedia article both aloud and in print with the students.

2. Students will be asked to summarize the article in three sentences and choose two extension questions from the list to answer about the passage.

Evaluation

Students will complete the "Questions to Myself Checklist" dealing with the information they have collected, sifted through, and are planning to use for their research reports.

Name: _____ Date: _____

Questions to Myself

Article Summary

_____

_____

_____

_____

Choose two of the following questions, underline your choices, and answer the questions in the space below.

- How does this information change what I think I know about this topic?
- Is this new information confusing?
- Is this new information different from other information I have collected?
- What do I still need to find out about my topic?

Answer to first question:

_____

_____

Answer to second question:

_____

_____

Name: _____ Date: _____

Questions to Myself Checklist

Use the questions below to guide you on your way as you continue to collect more information for your report.

1. How does this information change what I think I know?

2. How does this information fit in with other information I have collected?

3. Is this new information confusing?

4. Is this new information different from other information I have collected?

5. Does this information answer my thesis question?

6. What do I still need to find out about my topic?

7. Did I write down the bibliographic information about my topic?

Lesson Plan: In My Own Words

For the Teacher

One important skill that students should learn in the course of a research process is the skill of paraphrasing. They should practice reading information, thinking about it, and then putting the information into their own words.

Objectives

Students will learn the art of paraphrasing information to tailor it to their own needs.

The process of citation will be emphasized as an important part of the research process.

Materials

- "In My Own Words" worksheet (page 38)
- Encyclopedia article
- Overhead projector or computer display device

Procedures

1. The teacher will demonstrate the use of paraphrasing by sharing an encyclopedia article with the class and rewriting it to summarize and paraphrase information.

2. The teacher will also demonstrate the appropriate citation format for the encyclopedia article.

Evaluation

Students will read a portion of their collected research information and paraphrase the information to meet their stated thesis statement.
Students will correctly complete the appropriate citation format for their articles.

Name: _____ Date: _____

"In My Own Words"

Directions:

Read one of the articles or chapters that you have collected for your research.

Rewrite the article in your own words, paying close attention to your purpose in writing the report.

Don't forget to include a proper citation for the item you use to complete this assignment.

Information in your own words:

Citation for above information:

_____

Chapter 5: Searching for Information

Overview

When students begin to search for information on the Web, it is quickly apparent they need to learn effective searching skills. The use of directories, such as Yahooligans (http://www.yahooligans.com/), should be encouraged first, so students get an idea of what type of information is available on the Web. When older students need further information, they should be encouraged to use search engines, such as AltaVista and HotBot, for identifying potential sites of information that may be useful. They should be well versed in the advanced search strategies to help them limit the amount of unnecessary information they find.

The two lessons in this chapter, "The Internet Card Catalog" and "Search Engines and Mr. Boole," cover the basics of working with Internet directories and the large search engine databases.

Lesson Plan: The Internet Card Catalog

For the Teacher

The students will practice the skills of tunneling through a directory to see what types of information may be available about their topic.

Objective

Students will become familiar with the use of a directory to browse information.

Materials

- Computer and projection device
- "How Does a Directory Work?" handout (page 41)
- Access to a computer or computer lab
- "The Internet Card Catalog" worksheet (page 42)

Procedures

1. The teacher will explain that a directory is a group of sites, chosen by a person, which are categorized and cataloged similar to a library card catalog. The teacher will point out, however, that unlike a library card catalog, all the information on the Internet is not contained in any one directory. The teacher will go over the "How Does a Directory Work?" handout with the students.

2. The teacher will visit Yahooligans using a projection device. He/she will tunnel through one of the topics to get to a site via the subject headings route, then do a search in the search box to arrive at the same place. This will demonstrate to the students, the two methods of access to the information on the site.

3. Students will complete "The Internet Card Catalog" worksheet.

Evaluation

Students will successfully tunnel through a general directory to gather sites dealing with a topic.

How Does a Directory Work?

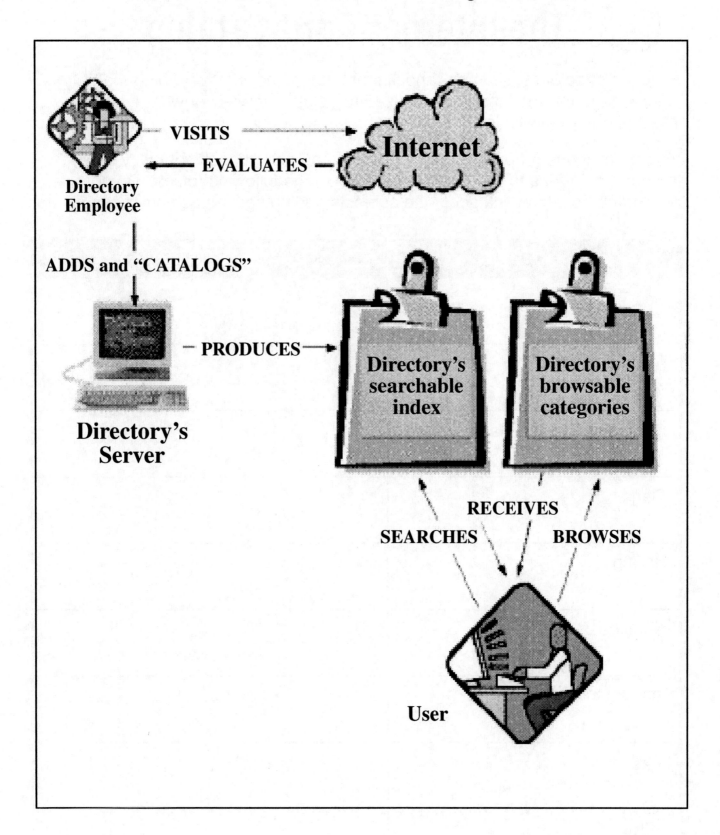

Name: _____ Date: _____

 # The Internet Card Catalog

Although directories, such as Yahooligans, do not include everything that is found on the Internet, they can be used to get an overview of what types of information are available.

Visit Yahooligans (http://www.yahooligans.com/) and "tunnel" your way down through the menus to find one site for each of the following topics. Do not use the search box, but think about the subjects and categories as you choose them.

TOPIC	SITE TITLE
Sea Turtles	
Beanie Babies™	
Computer & Video Games	
Flags	
Sailing	
Nutrition	
Instruments	
Magazines	
Software	

Lesson Plan: Search Engines and Mr. Boole

For the Teacher

The students will practice the skills of using advanced search strategies to limit the number of results obtained from the search engines.

Objective

Students will become familiar with the use of advanced search strategies.

Materials

- Computer and projection device
- "How Does a Search Engine Work?" handout (page 44)
- "Boolean Search Strategies" handout (page 45)
- Access to a computer or computer lab
- "Search Engines and Mr. Boole" worksheet (page 46)

Procedures

1. The teacher will explain that a search engine has two parts—a spider that collects information from Web servers and a database of information that the user is able to search. The teacher will go over the "How Does a Search Engine Work?" handout with the students.

2. The teacher will explain that George Boole, a philosopher and mathematician, designed a series of ways to explain how information can be related to other information. The strategies he came up with are today called Boolean search strategies. The teacher will cover the common strategies illustrated on the "Boolean Search Strategies" handout. The teacher will also point out that phrases should be enclosed in quotation marks in order to search them.

3. Students will complete their "Search Engines and Mr. Boole" worksheet.

Evaluation

Students will successfully use advanced search strategies to limit the number of search results on a topic when using a search engine.

How Does a Search Engine Work?

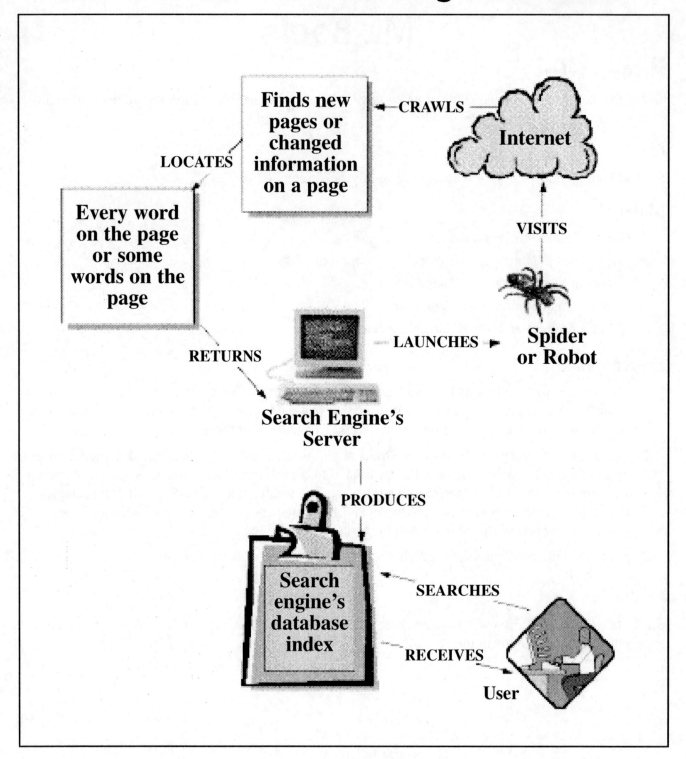

Name: _____ Date: _____

Boolean Search Strategies

How do I narrow a search using "and"?

- Using *and* will only provide links to sites which have BOTH of these words present

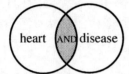

How do I narrow a search using "and"?

- Using *and* twice will limit the search even more

- You will only get pages that include all THREE of the terms

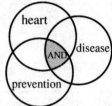

How do I broaden a search?

- Use of the word *or* will broaden a search

- Use *or* if two words may be used interchangeably

- Can use *or* more than once to get very broad

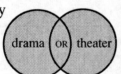

How do I narrow a search using "not"?

- Using *not* twice narrows the search be telling search engine to exclude certain words

- Alta Vista uses the form *and not*

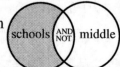

Name: _____ Date: _____

Search Engines and Mr. Boole

When using the search engines, it is best to start with the page that allows you to use some Boolean search strategies to limit or broaden your search.

Go to AltaVisa (http://altavista.com), type the term(s) on line A, and record the number of results that are returned for each entry. Then choose the *Advanced Search* menu item and type the term(s) on line B in the large search box, as written, and record the number of results obtained with this type of search for each entry.

Terms to Search	Number of Results
Line A: endangered species	
Line B: endangered and owls	
Line A: middle school	
Line B: middle school and students	
Line A: cars	
Line B: cars and Toyota	
Line A: toys	
Line B: toys or games	

1. What can you predict about the number of results that will be returned for the advanced searches?

_____

2. Why is this true?

_____

_____

_____

Chapter 6: Evaluating the Information

Overview

In this era of information overload, students need to be able to separate the valid information from the incorrect information, recognize the authority from which an author speaks, and realize whether information is useful for their particular purpose.

The National Educational Technology Standards project (NETS), proposed by the International Society for Technology in Education (ISTE) as the basis for technology literacy for students in grades K–12, outlines several standards that encompass critical evaluation of information. Two standards, listed under the use of technology as a research tool, are: "students (will) use technology to locate, evaluate, and collect information from a variety of sources (and) evaluate and select new information resources and technological innovations based on the appropriateness to specific tasks." This important document is finding its way into many of the states' curriculum frameworks and guidelines documents as a common thread that needs to be addressed across disciplines. The full text of the NETS document may be found at http://cnets.iste.org/.

The two lessons in this chapter, "You Be the Judge!" and "The 5 W's of Web Site Evaluation," are intended to help students learn to look at information with a critical eye. By working with students to make them aware of the types of things to look for when evaluating a site, they will be learning the lifelong skill of critical evaluation of information.

Lesson Plan: You Be the Judge!

For the Teacher

Evaluation of information can only occur when students have a working knowledge base about a topic and are able to determine whether the information that they find is true based on this knowledge base. The following is a fun lesson that is intended to demonstrate to students that all the information that they find on the Web may not be true.

Objective

Students will investigate and determine whether information found on the Internet is valid.

Materials

- Access to a computer with an Internet connection, preferably in a lab situation
- "You Be the Judge!" worksheet (page 49)
- Computer projection device

Procedures

1. The teacher will demonstrate the use of one of the student directories (e.g., Yahooligans, Eblast, Homework Helper) to show the students how to browse the categories.

2. Students will be asked to choose a hobby or topic of interest to them, browse the directory for information, and look at various sites dealing with the topic.

3. Students will compare and contrast information found on these sites and complete the "You Be the Judge!" worksheet.

4. The teacher will lead a discussion dealing with the results of their findings.

Evaluation

Students will come up with one or more facts from the investigated sites that they feel are false.
Students will complete the "You Be the Judge!" worksheet.
Students will discuss why they think incorrect information appears on the Internet.

Name: _____ Date: _____

You Be the Judge!

Choose a topic that you know a lot about and are interested in. Browse through the directory that your teacher instructs you to use and find some sites about your topic.

Look carefully at the information on the different sites. Is there information that is different on some of them? Is there information that you know is wrong on some of them?

Write down the URL (Web page address) of any site on which you find incorrect information. Explain what the wrong information is. At the end of the lesson, you will be asked to talk about why you think you might find incorrect information on the Internet.

My Topic: _____

URL: _____

Incorrect Information:_____

_____

URL: _____

Incorrect Information:_____

_____

Lesson Plan: The 5 W's of Web Site Evaluation

For the Teacher

Evaluation of Internet information takes a multi-tiered approach. At the simplest level, students can use a checklist to determine whether the information that they find is easy to use, authoritative, and applicable to their purpose. The following lesson can help teach students about the triggers they should be looking for when evaluating a Web site.

Objective

Students will become familiar with some of the aspects of evaluating Web sites.

Materials

- "The 5 W's of Web Site Evaluation" slide show transparencies (pages 53-58)
- Overhead projector and overhead transparencies
- "The 5 W's for Evaluating Web Sites Information Sheet" (page 59)
- Evaluation sheets for each student (elementary, middle, or advanced) (pages 60-65)
- Large screen projection device, computer, and Internet access

Procedures

1. The teacher will first show the series of transparencies and explain the rationale for each of the criteria of Web site evaluation to the students.

2. Together, the teacher will lead the class through a formal evaluation of a chosen Web site, talking about the various items to look for when evaluating a site and using the student evaluation sheet.

3. Students will then complete evaluation sheets for each of the Web sites they will be using for their projects.

Evaluation

Students will complete an evaluation sheet for each one of the sites that they are using for their research.

The 5 W's of Web Site Evaluation

The following are small versions of the overhead slides and information to go along with each one.

Who? What? When? Where? Why? 5 W's of Web Site Evaluation	Explain to students the importance of thinking carefully about the information that appears on a Web site. Let them know that the traditional who, what, when, where, and why questions will lead them to easily evaluate a site.
Who? Who wrote the pages and is he/she an expert? Is a biography of the author of the site included? How can you find out more about the author?	Explain that the authority of the author is always an important piece. If a biography of an author is included, this makes it easier, but there should also be a way to contact the author for further information whether by e-mail or regular mail. Searching the online library card catalogs and large bookstore offerings will also indicate if the author has written any published books on the topic.
What? What does the author say is the purpose of the site? What else might the author have in mind for the site? What makes this site easy to use?	Every good Web site includes a rationale for why the site was created and why the author chose to include certain types of information. The navigation of the site is also an important aspect which aids the students with ease of use and should be addressed with them.

The 5 W's of Web Site Evaluation *(cont.)*

When was the site created?

When was the site last updated?

All good Web sites include the date they were created and the date the site was last updated. This is very important in an area of frequent and rapid development, like cloning, the space program, or negotiations in the Middle East. Students who are working on topics that change should be encouraged to visit these types of sites frequently to get the latest information.

Where does the information come from?

Where can I look to find out more about the producer of the page?

If a bibliography of sources used by the Web page author is included, students have an easy way to verify the information on their own.
However, if there are no citations, as stated before, students should have the information needed to contact the author and ask for further information.

Why is the information useful for my purpose?

Why should I use this information?

Why is this page better than another?

After examining the information found, students should assess whether the information is useful for the purpose of their research paper. They should also be able to justify why they are choosing one piece of information over another and using one particular page instead of another.
This can only be accomplished after acquiring a knowledge base on the topic at hand and widely investigating Web sites and print sources.

Who? What? When? Where? Why?

5 W's of Web Site Evaluation

WHO?

Who wrote the pages and is he/she an expert?

Is a biography of the author of the site included?

How can you find out more about the author?

What

What does the author say is the purpose of the site?

What else might the author have in mind for the site?

What makes this site easy to use?

When

When was the site created?

When was the site last updated?

Where?

Where does the information come from?

Where can I look to find out more about the producer of the page?

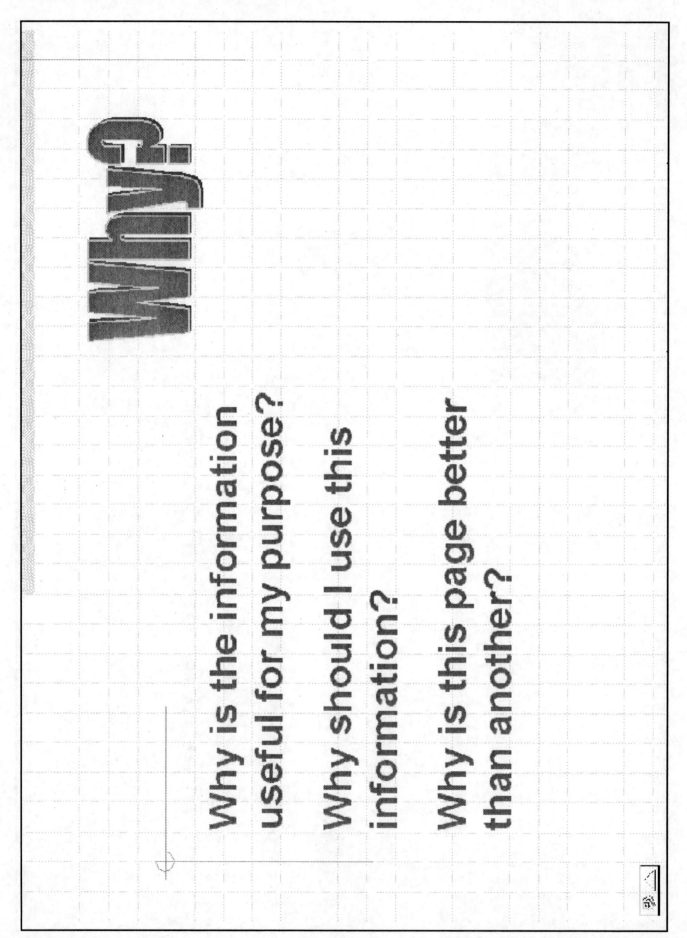

Why?

Why is the information useful for my purpose?

Why should I use this information?

Why is this page better than another?

Name: _____ Date: _____

The 5 W's for Evaluating Web Sites

Who	Who wrote the pages and is he/she an expert? Is a biography of the author included? How can you find out more about the author?
What	What does the author say is the purpose of the site? What else might the author have in mind for the site? What makes the site easy to use?
When	When was the site created? When was the site last updated?
Where	Where does the information come from? Where can I look to find out more about the producer of the page?
Why	Why is this information useful for my purpose? Why should I use this information? Why is this page better than another?

W W W W W

Name: _____ Date: _____

Critical Evaluation of a Web Site: Elementary School Level

©1996 Kathleen Schrock (kschrock@capecod.net)
Kathy Schrock's Guide for Educators—http://discoveryschool.com/schrockguide/

Circle or write in your response as appropriate.

1. How are you connected to the Internet?

    _____ Computer and modem   _____ Direct connection at school

2. If you are using a modem, what is the speed?

    2400   9600   14.4K   28.8K   33.6K   56K

3. What Web browser are you using? _____

4. What is the URL of the Web page you are looking at?

    http:// _____

5. What is the name of the site? _____

How Does It Look?

1. Does the page take a long time to load?   YES   NO

2. Are there big pictures on the page?   YES   NO

3. Is the spelling correct on the page?   YES   NO

4. Is the author's name and e-mail address on the page?   YES   NO

5. Is there a picture on the page that you can use to choose links? (Image map) YES   NO

6. Is information on the page in columns? (Table)   YES   NO

7. If you go to another page, is there a way to get back to the first page?   YES   NO

8. Is there a date that tells you when the page was made?   YES   NO

9. Do the photographs look real?   YES   NO   NO PHOTOGRAPHS

10. Do the sounds sound real?   YES   NO   NO SOUND

Critical Evaluation of a Web Site: Elementary School Level *(cont.)*

What Did You Learn?

Circle the correct response.

1. Does the title of the page tell you what it is about?   YES   NO

2. Is there an introduction on the page that tells you what is included?   YES   NO

3. Are the facts on the page what you were looking for?   YES   NO

4. Would you have gotten more information from the encyclopedia?   YES   NO

5. Would the information have been better in the encyclopedia?   YES   NO

6. Does the author of the page say some things you disagree with?   YES   NO

7. Does the author of the page include information that you know is wrong?   YES   NO

8. Do the pictures and photographs on the page help you learn?   YES   NO   NO PICTURES

Summary

Looking at all of the questions and answers above, write a paragraph telling why this Web site is helpful to you for your project.

_____

_____

_____

_____

_____

_____

_____

_____

URL of this page: http://discoveryschool.com/schrockguide/evalelem.html

Name: _____ Date: _____

Critical Evaluation of a Web Site: Middle School Level

©1996 Kathleen Schrock (kschrock@capecod.net)
Kathy Schrock's Guide for Educators—http://discoveryschool.com/schrockguide

Circle or write in your response as appropriate.

1. What type of connection do you have to the Internet?

    _____ Dial-in access: modem speed   2400   9600   14.4K   28.8K   33.6K   56K

    _____ Direct connection: 56K   T1   T3   other: _____

2. What Web browser are you using? _____

3. What is the URL of the Web page you are evaluating?

    http:// _____

4. What is the name of the site? _____

Part One: Looking At and Using the Page

Circle the correct response.

1. Does the page take a long time to load?	YES	NO
2. Are the pictures on the page helpful?	YES NO	NOT APPLICABLE
3. Is each section of the page labeled with a heading?	YES	NO
4. Did the author sign his/her real name?	YES	NO
5. Did the author give you his/her e-mail address?	YES	NO
6. Is there a date on the page that tells you when it was last updated?	YES	NO
7. Is there an image map (big picture with links) on the page?	YES	NO
8. Is there a table (columns of text) on the page? (Check the source code.)	YES	NO
9. If so, is the table readable with your browser?	YES	NO
10. If you go to another page on the site, can you get back to the main page?	YES	NO
11. Are there photographs on the page?	YES	NO
12. If so, can you be sure that the author has not changed photographs?	YES	NO
13. If you're not sure, should you accept the photos as true?	YES	NO

Critical Evaluation of a Web Site:
Middle School Level *(cont.)*

Summary of Part One

Using the data you have collected above, write a paragraph explaining why you would or would not recommend this site to a friend for use with a project.

_____

_____

_____

_____

_____

_____

_____

_____

Part Two: What's on the Page and Who Put It There?

1. Does the title of the page tell you what it is about? YES NO

2. Is there a paragraph on the page explaining what it is about? YES NO

3. Is the information on the page useful for your project? YES NO

   If not, what can you do next? _____

4. Would you have gotten more information from an encyclopedia? YES NO

5. Is the information on the page current? YES NO

6. Does up-to-date information make a difference for your project? YES NO

7. Does the page lead you to some other good information (links)? YES NO

8. Does the author of the page present some information you disagree with? YES NO

9. Does the author of the page present some information that you think is wrong? YES NO

10. Does some information contradict information you found elsewhere? YES NO

11. Does the author use some absolute words like "always" or "never"? YES NO

12. Does the author use superlative words like the "best" or "worst"? YES NO

Critical Evaluation of a Web Site:
Middle School Level *(cont.)*

13. Does the author tell you about him/herself?   YES   NO

14. Do you feel that the author is knowledgeable about the topic?   YES   NO

15. Are you positive the information is true?   YES   NO

16. What can you do to prove the information is true?

_____

_____

_____

Summary of Part Two

Looking at the data you have collected in part two, compose a note to the author of the Web site explaining how you are going to use the Web site in your project and what your opinion is of the page's content.

_____

_____

_____

_____

_____

_____

_____

_____

_____

_____

URL of this page: http://discoveryschool.com/schrockguide/evalmidd.html

Name: _____ Date: _____

Critical Evaluation of a Web Site: Advanced Level

Location
URL of the page http://
Name of the page:

Technical and Visual Aspects of the Web Page
Does the page take a long time to load?
Are any important pictures labeled with a caption?
Is the spelling correct on the page?
Are there headings and subheadings on the page? Are they helpful?
Is the page signed by the author?
Is the author's e-mail address included?
Is there a date of last update? Is the date current?
Is the format standard and readable with your browser?
Is there an image map (large clickable graphic w/ hyperlinks) on the page?
Is there a table on the page? Is the table readable with your browser?
If you have graphics turned off, is there a text alternate to the images?
On supporting pages, is there a link back to the home page?
Are the links clearly visible and explanatory?
Is there a picture or a sound included? Can you be sure it has not been edited?
Should you accept the information as valid for your purpose?

Content
Does the title of the page indicate the content?
Is the purpose of the page indicated on the home page?
When was the document created?
Is the information useful for your purpose?
Would it have been easier to get the information somewhere else?
Would information somewhere else have been different? Why?
Did the information lead you to other sources that were useful?
Is a bibliography of print sources included?
Is the information current if that is important to your purpose?
Does the information appear biased because of the use of certain words?
Does the information contradict something you found somewhere else?
Do most of the pictures supplement the content of the page?

Authority
Is it easy to tell who created the page?
Can you tell with what organization the person is affiliated?
Has the site been reviewed by an online/print-reviewing agency?
Does the domain (i.e., edu, com, gov) of the page influence your evaluation of the site?
Are you positive that the information is true? How can you prove it?
Can you verify the information in a reputable print source?
Are you satisfied that the information is useful for your purpose?

© 1998 Kathleen Schrock kschrock@capecod.net

Chapter 7: Utilizing the People on the Internet

Overview

Besides the Web sites that are chock full of information to support the research process, there are two other methods of gathering information from the Internet—asking an expert for help and searching the newsgroups.

The easy access to people is one of the great things about the Internet. People in the work force are often willing to answer a question for a student who is working on a report, especially if the student has completed a thorough research process before asking the question.

Ask-An-Expert Sites

There are many sites available which are set up to allow students to ask a question of an expert in the field. These sites are easy to find although the answer may take a bit of time to get back since they are also heavily used. It would be helpful to bookmark these sites on the classroom computer to allow students access to the experts who might be needed for their research project.

Some of the best known of these sites include:

Ask-An-Expert Page http://njnie.dl.stevens-tech.edu/askanexpert.html
Electronic Emissary http://emissary.ots.utexas.edu/emissary/index.html
Pitsco's Ask an Expert Page http://www.askanexpert.com
XpertSite.com http://www.XpertSite.com/

Newsgroups

The newsgroups include the postings of millions of individuals to thousands of newsgroups on various topics. Some of the material in the newsgroups may not be appropriate for elementary or middle school students. It's best to monitor the archive searching of the newsgroups by students.

The main site that archives the newsgroup postings is:

Google Groups
http://groups.google.com

Specifically Newsgroups
http://groups.google.com/groups?group=news&hl=en

Lesson Plan: News for All

For the Teacher

The newsgroups on the Internet include a wealth of information from both experts and interested individuals. By allowing access to the large archive of recent postings, students can find information that may support their research theses.

Objective

Students will search the newsgroups for information on a topic.

Materials

- Access to a computer with an Internet connection, preferably in a lab situation
- "News for All" worksheet (page 68)
- Computer projection device

Procedures

1. The teacher will explain that the newsgroups are similar to a bulletin board where people post questions and other people post answers. The teacher should point out that everyone with Internet access has the ability to post answers, and all answers should be verified. Students should be reminded that they should follow up on answers they have some question about by conducting further research.

2. The teacher will visit the Deja.com site and walk the students through an advanced search on a topic. The teacher will point out the various parts of each returned result including the date of posting, the title of the article, the newsgroup posted to, the items which are responses to a previous post, and the poster of the message.

3. Students will complete the "News for All" worksheet.

Evaluation

Students will search the newsgroup archives to come up with conflicting or untrue information.

Name: _____ Date: _____

News for All

Below is a sample of the results from a newsgroup search on a person's name.

Date ▾	Subject ▾	Forum ▾	Author ▾
02/18/1999	Kathy Schrock's Guide for Ed	k12.ed.art	Kathleen Schroc
01/02/1999	Kathy Schrock's Guide for Ed	k12.chat.teacher	Kathy Schrock
06/01/1999	Re: Weirdness in Palm Deskto	alt comp.sys.palmtops	Kathy Schrock
05/31/1999	Weirdness in Palm Desktop	alt comp.sys.palmtops	Kathy Schrock
12/22/1998	Kathy Schrock's Guide moves!	Sch.sig.imnet	Kathy Schrock

A. What can you possibly tell about Kathy Schrock's interests from these postings?

_____

B. Draw a circle around the posting which is a response to another posting.

C. Visit the Deja.com Power Search page
   http://x38.deja.com/=rd/home_ps.shtml

   Type the following phrase into the keyword search box and examine the resulting list to answer the following questions.

   > *cake recipes*

   1. Which newsgroup would you most likely monitor to find out more about this topic? Why did you choose that newsgroup?

   _____

   2. Does it seem as if this is a very active newsgroup with many members? How can you tell?

   _____

Chapter 8: Information Retrieval Skills System

Overview

Jan Wahlers and Mary Watkins have designed a step-by-step research approach that may be applied across the curriculum entitled the *Information Retrieval Skills* system (IRS). The goal of the IRS is to help students develop research skills in a hassle free environment.

Many of the lessons in this book may be used to supplement the IRS model. The model encompasses more of the traditional research processes, and does not directly address the use of a computer for research or Web site evaluation as outlined in the previous chapters. However, the traditional research model presented in the IRS, in conjunction with the computer-based research process presented in this book, would make a powerful combination which would lead to the student acquisition of research skills.

The IRS is divided into 12 separate steps. Each of these will be covered on the following pages.

Step 1:   Topic Selection

Step 2:   Library Research Using Search Strategy Forms

Step 3:   Narrowing and Focusing the Topic

Step 4:   Preliminary Outline

Step 5:   Thesis Statements (or Thesis Questions)

Step 6:   Gathering Information

Step 7:   Note Cards

Step 8:   Sentence Outline

Step 9:   Parenthetical Footnotes

Step 10:   Writing the First Draft

Step 11:   Revising and Writing the Final Draft

Step 12:   Works Cited Page

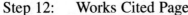

Name: _____ Date: _____

Information Retrieval Skills System

Step 1: Topic Selection

Think about what interests you. You might ask other people for ideas about topics in areas of your interest. This step is important because you will be spending a great deal of time with this topic.

Avoid trivial topics. You will need to prove a thesis statement or answer a thesis question. Remember, you must PROVE something. This is what makes a research paper different from a report.

Understand the limits of the assignment in terms of time required to thoroughly cover the topic. It is better to cover a narrow topic completely than to lightly touch on many aspects of a general topic.

Understand the resource limitations. An excuse that you could not find enough material means that you should have chosen a different topic.

My ideas for my topic are:

_____

_____

_____

The question(s) I am trying to answer include:

_____

_____

_____

_____

Name: _____ Date: _____

Step 2: Library Research Using Search Strategy Forms

Few architects or engineers would begin building without a blueprint or a set of master plans. However, a great deal of research is started and conducted with no planning. A search strategy is an organized plan of action for researching. Use the Search Strategy 1 and 2 forms (pages 72 and 74) to help you keep track of all your sources as you research. These forms will also help your teacher know where you have looked for information and whether your keywords are too general or too specific. By using Search Strategy forms, instructors are able to monitor the progress of an entire class of researchers quickly and easily. When you have a question for your teacher, bring your Search Strategy form with you.

Search Strategy 1 Directions

Follow these examples when filling out the Search Strategy 1 Form.

1. **Topic:** This line should contain your research topic.
2. **Thesis:** This is what you want to know about your topic.
3. **Revised thesis:** If you can't find any information, you might wish to change your topic, check your spelling, or shift the research focus.

   Example: Narrowing the topic from *Egypt* to *Nile River* or expanding from *Hammerhead sharks* to *Sharks*.
4. **Keywords B:** The first column should be filled out *before* beginning library research. List all the words associated with your topic that you can think of.

   For example, using Egypt as a topic: B=Nile, pyramids, King Tut
5. **Keywords K:** The second column is used after your research begins. Add subjects and terms (*k*eywords) that you discover in your search.

   For example, using Egypt as a topic: Egypt K=Alexander the Great, Cleopatra, Sphinx
6. **Keywords CR:** *C*ommunity *R*esources. The third column is for contacts and resources outside of the library.

   For example, using Egypt as a topic: CR= personal interviews at the Nile Restaurant, museum exhibit, etc.

At the bottom of the "Search Strategy 1 Form," there are two boxes that will allow you to list where you might find information on the keywords listed in the K and CR columns.

Name: _____ Date: _____

Search Strategy 1 Form

Follow the directions on the previous page in order to fill this page out correctly. Notice that the top portion needs to be completed before beginning to research.

Search Strategy 1: Keywords (SS1)		
Topic: _____		
Thesis: _____		
Revised thesis: _____		
KEYWORDS—B List keywords before starting your research.	**KEYWORDS—K** List other words that lead you to information on your topic.	**KEYWORDS—CR** List community resources, Internet, businesses, public libraries, museums.
	Where to find the keywords in this column:	Where to find the keywords in this column:

Name: _____ Date: _____

Step 2: Library Research Using Search Strategy Forms *(cont.)*

▪▪

Search Strategy 2 Directions

1. Transfer the top information from SS1 (Topic, Thesis, Revised Thesis) onto the SS2 log.

2. List every place you look for information. Record enough information so that you can find the source again, if needed.

3. If information is located in the listed source, place a plus sign (+) in the space marked "Hit." If you did not locate information in the source, place a zero (0) in the box and a minus sign (-) in the "Hit" space.

4. If more room is needed, use an additional form. It is not unusual to have 20 to 50 listings on a topic!

Name: _____ Date: _____

Search Strategy 2 Log

▨▨▨▨▨▨▨▨▨▨▨▨▨▨▨▨▨▨▨▨▨▨▨▨▨▨▨▨▨▨▨

Follow the directions on the previous page in order to fill this page out correctly. Notice that the top portion needs to be completed before beginning to research.

Search Strategy 2 Log	
Topic:_____	
Thesis: _____	
Revised thesis: _____	
Source, keyword, and other information	**Hit**
Example: World Book Encyclopedia 1996 K=Egypt "Ancient Egypt" by Leonard H. Lesko, p. 345	+
Page _____ of _____	

Name: _____ Date: _____

Step 2: Library Research Using Search Strategy Forms *(cont.)*

▪▪

Using the Internet

When using the Internet for a class project or assignment, it is important to identify the contact site or place of access on the Search Strategy Form. Therefore, the first part of your entry should look like these sample entries:

1. Library > Netscape

2. Lab 225 > Netscape

3. Home computer > AOL

4. Indianapolis Public Library > Netscape

5. Bracken Library, Ball State University > Netscape

6. Dad's office (use name) > AOL

▪▪

Accessing a Direct Web Site

Search Strategy Sample:

Library > Netscape > www.discovery.com
K=hurricanes
Comment: great source

If this information is used in the assignment, the citation would be:

"Rage of Hurricane Floyd." Discovery Channel. 16 Sept. 1999. Netscape.
      Available: http://www.discovery.com/

Step 2: Library Research Using Search Strategy Forms *(cont.)*

Documenting When Using a Search Engine

Sample:
Home computer > Netscape > SNAP
K=hurricanes
Comment: 12 pages/ National Hurricane Center (good info)

If this information is used in the assignment, the citation would be:

"Active Storm Advisories." National Hurricane Center. 19 September 1999

Netscape. Available: http//www.nhc.noaa.gov/

Extending the Search or Use Different Keywords Within the Same Source

Sample:
Home computer > Netscape > SNAP
K= hurricanes
    Comment: 12 pages / National Hurricane Center (good info)
K= hurricane safety
    Comment: 1 page (3 out of 4 URLs not available)
K= hurricane hunters
    Comment: 1 page
K= Hurricane Hugo

Changing Search Engines or Directories

More keywords may be added under this entry as long as the searcher stays in SNAP. If the searcher changes search engines, then another entry is required. The same keywords could be used. It might look like this:

Sample: Home computer > Netscape > Excite
K= hurricanes
    Comment: 240 hits /commercial products and sport teams also listed
K= hurricane safety
    Comment: 29 hits including what color of Honda Hurricane to buy
K= hurricane hunters
    Comment: 100 hits, several in foreign languages

Name: _____ Date: _____

Step 3: Narrowing and Focusing the Topic

Choose your narrowed topic according to the question that most interests you. You may want to combine two very specific questions together if you can't find enough information on your specific topic.

Make sure that you will be able to find enough information on your topic to write a research paper!

Be sure that you avoid huge topics such as *China or World War II* if you will be writing a relatively short paper or making a short presentation. It is far better to fully cover a narrow topic than to partially investigate a large or general topic.

Step 4: Preliminary Outline

A preliminary outline is nothing more than a road map which will help focus on what information is needed. You may decide to change the focus of the report later, after researching the topic, but for now, the working or preliminary outline will provide direction.

Example of a preliminary outline

Topic: Experiments performed by Nazis during WWII
Thesis: Nazis performed many experiments on prisoners during WWII
  I. Genetic experiments
  II. Physical experiments
  III. Psychological experiments

One of the subtopics (I, II, III) will go on the top of each note card. By putting a subtopic on the top of each card, your work will be cut in half later when it's time to write the sentence outline and first draft.

Name: _____ Date: _____

Step 5: Thesis Statements (or Thesis Questions)

1. Identify a specific topic that most interests you.

2. In order to write a thesis question, you will need to answer one main question (thesis question) about this topic. This question should be one that you don't already know the answer to, or a question that has no readily apparent answer.

3. After writing a thesis question (often the first step in determining a thesis statement), you will need to convert this question into a statement. This will be the statement that you will prove with research. Remember that the research may end up disproving the thesis statement. This is just fine. You may choose to rewrite the thesis statement even after you have finished the research or come to the conclusion, after reviewing all the evidence, that the thesis statement was wrong.

4. When writing a thesis statement, be sure to reflect a formal tone. Avoid using slang or words that suggest an informal, personal tone (such as "I think . . ." or "In my opinion . . .").

5. The thesis statement or question should tell the readers what you intend to prove.

6. The thesis statement or question must be in the first paragraph of the research paper.

Name: _____ Date: _____

Step 5: Thesis Statements (or Thesis Questions) *(cont.)*

▪▪▪

Often, beginning researchers have a problem figuring out how to write a thesis statement. A thesis statement is to a research paper what a topic sentence is to a paragraph. A topic sentence describes what the paragraph will be about, while the thesis statement explains what the writer intends to prove in that paper. When writing a five-paragraph essay, students should also have a thesis statement. The thesis statement for longer pieces of writing such as essays or research papers needs to let the reader know what the writer intends to prove.

A thesis statement is a complete declarative sentence, which is composed of a subject that identifies the topic of the paper and a predicate that shows the writer's attitude about that same topic. It is possible that you may want to modify the thesis statement upon the completion of research or after the first draft. This is perfectly acceptable, but you need to make sure that all of the information presented in the paper helps prove the thesis statement. Avoid adding information that is interesting but does not help prove the thesis statement.

▪▪▪

A thesis statement should not be one of the following . . .

- A well-known fact that can be shown to be true. This is common knowledge that needs no researching.

    Example: American soldiers fought Germans in WWII.

- A biased opinion that can't be proven.

    Example: Yorktown, Indiana is the best place to vacation in the U.S.

- A personal statement about which you can write entirely from your own knowledge or experience.

    Example: I have been collecting baseball cards for two years.

Name: _____ Date: _____

Step 5: Thesis Statements (or Thesis Questions) *(cont.)*

■▬■

The thesis statement may . . .

- claim that there is a problem.

    Example: Many women experienced problems after WWII when their jobs were given to returning GI's.

- offer a solution to a problem.

    Example: Cities could solve their waste disposal problems by making better use of recycling.

- reveal that there is a new development.

    Example: The use of a modem has dramatically increased a student's ability to conduct research and receive information from overseas.

- state a conclusion that you have reached after completing your research.

    Example: In the future, computers will change the record-keeping practices of American families.

■▬■

Sample Thesis Statements

1. Eating green vegetables can significantly reduce the risk of colon cancer.

2. Salvador Dali's paintings reveal events, people, and ideas in symbolic forms.

3. Certain forms of exercise may be detrimental to elementary students.

4. Acupuncture is a widely accepted form of medical treatment in certain parts of the world.

5. During the Civil War, the South had many military advantages over the North.

6. It is possible, within certain parameters, to predict the location of earthquakes.

7. Nuclear power is essential to the defense of the United States.

Name: _____ Date: _____

Step 6: Gathering Information

As you look for information, keep in mind that you want only those sources that can prove the thesis or provide answers to one of the questions. As tempted as you may be to use other related information, use only the information that answers the thesis question or proves the thesis statement. Be sure to skim the article before taking notes to be sure that it contains the information you're looking for.

Source Cards

Source cards are used to keep track of all the sources (encyclopedias, books, interviews, magazines, Web pages, etc.) that are used during research.

As soon as you have found a source that you plan to use, make a source card. On this source card, write all the bibliographic information needed for the works cited page. (The works cited page is another name for the bibliography.)

In order to keep source cards separate and in order, they should be numbered in the upper left-hand corner. All note cards written from this source will have the same number (but a different letter) on the top left of the card (example: 1a, 1b, and 1c would go on all note cards from source one). By numbering source and note cards, a student always knows which source the information came from. Numbering cards is necessary later when writing parenthetical footnotes to give the original authors credit.

In the upper right-hand corner, put the call number (or Web page address) and the source where you obtained this resource, so you or your teacher may check your information.

Name: _____ Date: _____

Step 6: Gathering Information *(cont.)*

▮▰

Writing Source Cards

A source card identifies a research source. After writing a source card, begin taking notes from this source on note cards. The information required on a source card includes the following: the name of the source, the citation information, a number that corresponds to the number on all the note cards from that source, the call number (or URL), the location of the library or source of the information, and a comment about what is located in the source (in case you want to go back and get additional information).

Sometimes publications do not present all the information needed for the source card. You must not invent information. You should only use the information that is available. For example, in some sources such as the Internet, page numbers cannot be used.

All source cards have a number, library or location of the source, bibliographical information, and a comment. However, each citation (the author, name of the book, city of publication, etc.) will be slightly different. Be sure to use the "Menu for Success" handout (pages 22–23) to look up the correct form for each of your sources. Notice the order in which the information must be presented.

▮▰

Sample Source Card for a Book

```
1                                          808
                                           DYH Library
Twain, Mark.  The Adventures of Tom Sawyer.  New York: Holt-
Rinehart, 1998.
Comment: Good source for local color on Mississippi River.
```

Name: _____ Date: _____

Step 7: Note Cards

1. Using a 3" x 5" or 4" x 6" file card, write the number of the source in the upper left-hand corner.

2. After the source number, letter each note card from that source with a different letter.

3. Reduce the information to short phrases. Avoid copying information directly from the source unless it is a direct quotation. Be sure to place quotation marks around direct quotes.

4. Begin a new note card for each new piece of information.

5. It is important to summarize the information in your own words.

6. At the bottom of each note card, place the page number where you found this information.

7. Place the topic covered on that particular note card at the top of the card. This will be beneficial when sorting the information.

Important Note: Plagiarism, using another writer's words or ideas as if they were your own, is a serious offense. Any time you use exact words from a source or paraphrase words or ideas, it is important to credit the source.

Name: _____ Date: _____

Step 7: Note Cards *(cont.)*

▪▪

Note Card Organization

7A   THE SUBTOPIC GOES HERE

Notes go here

Use summaries, direct quotations, etc.

Each idea has its own note card

No sentences

Take notes

Page number of information from source goes here

Remember that each note card has one subtopic at the top of the card. This allows you to know how to categorize the specific notes on this card. You wouldn't place notes about the emotional effects of the bombing of Hiroshima on the same note card as, for example, information about the long-term health problems of those who survived the bombing of Hiroshima.

▪▪

Note-taking Methods

1. **Summary:** Condensing long passages into just the facts and ideas will save time writing! Use this method most often.

2. **Paraphrase:** To paraphrase means to put someone else's words into your own words. It is generally longer than a summary because you are "translating" the author's work. Paraphrasing must be footnoted.

3. **Direct Quotation:** Use sparingly and only when it is crucial to keep the author's exact original wording. Copy the quotation word for word and enclose it in quotation marks.

Name: _____ Date: _____

Step 8: Sentence Outline

▰▰▰▰▰▰▰▰▰▰▰▰▰▰▰▰▰▰▰▰▰▰▰▰▰▰▰▰▰▰▰▰▰▰▰▰▰▰

The MLA (Modern Language Association) style requires a researcher to write a full sentence outline. This outline is to be placed immediately before a research paper. Each heading, subheading, etc. must be written in a complete sentence.

Using the method for taking notes described in Step 7 will make outlining your report much easier. Make an outline before writing the paper. Unless major changes are made, the final sentence outline will be an extension of the preliminary outline.

After you've finished taking notes, group note cards with similar ideas in piles, according to the heading at the top of the card. The note card subtopic headings become the main headings (noted by capitalized Roman numerals I, II, III, etc.) of the sentence outline. The information on the cards becomes the supporting points under each main outline heading. Notes should be logically organized under the appropriate headings.

▰▰▰▰▰▰▰▰▰▰▰▰▰▰▰▰▰▰▰▰▰▰▰▰▰▰▰▰▰▰▰▰▰▰▰▰▰▰

Sentence Outline Form

1. Use Roman numerals for main topics.

2. Use capital letters for subtopics.

3. Always include at least two subtopics under each main topic. If you include supporting points under a subtopic, include at least two.

4. Line up all the subtopics, points, sub-points, etc. Indent, as in the model sentence outline "Oodles of Outlines" (page 33).

5. Capitalize the first word of each outline entry.

6. Use complete sentences in the sentence outline, except for the heading.

Name: _____ Date: _____

Step 9: Parenthetical Footnotes

When you put information in the paper gained from a source, give credit to the author. You need to indicate to the reader the source of the information. Facts that are common knowledge need not be cited. List sources for direct quotes, ideas that were paraphrased, and sources for figures and statistics.

A parenthetical footnote is a short reference (in parentheses) in the body of the report. It refers readers to the entry on the works cited page at the end of the paper. It has the author's name and the page number or numbers where the information was found.

A citation within the body of a report consists of the author's last name and the page number or numbers on which the information is found, for example (Jones 356–357). Do not list all the pages of the entire article as you did on the source cards. Cite the pages used for this particular bit of information. Use no punctuation between the author's name and the page number. If there is no author, abbreviate the title of the source.

If a quotation of five or more lines is used, indent the quotation as a block, 10 spaces from the left margin of the report. Do not enclose the quotation in quotation marks. Place the citation, in parentheses, at the end of the quotation after the final period.

Sample Parenthetical Footnotes

Parenthetical footnote:

The following magazine citation omits the author's name because the author's name is mentioned in the text.

Barrett states that "D-Day was almost postponed due to the interference of poor weather conditions" (37).

Parenthetical footnote within the text:

During WWII, the government of Japan agreed to sign an unconditional surrender after the second atomic bomb was dropped on their country (Barrett 10–12).

*Notice how the end punctuation is placed after the parenthetical footnote!

Name: _____ Date: _____

Step 10: Writing the First Draft

▚▚▚

Use the outline to write the paper. In writing the first draft, the goal is to organize and develop the ideas and to get those ideas down on paper. In later drafts, you will revise and polish your ideas as well as revise the wording and proofread for errors. Your paper must not simply string the sentences of the sentence outline together. You will be doing the thinking and writing using your own words.

▚▚▚

Introductory Paragraph

Begin the report with an introduction. These first few sentences should be some interesting information about the topic that will grab the reader's attention. For a short report, the introduction is usually one paragraph. The introductory paragraph consists of two or three sentences that lead up to the thesis statement (or thesis question). It is best not to make the first sentence the thesis statement. After reading the introductory paragraph, readers should know what the report will be about. Since this is a formal paper, do not use informal language or personal pronouns (for example, "I am going to write about . . .").

▚▚▚

Body

The body of the report supports and develops the thesis statement. Follow the outline to write the body of the report. Use the Roman numeral headings and the lettered subheadings of the outline to form the topic sentence for each paragraph. Some lettered and numbered subheadings of the outline will be used to form the important supporting details of each paragraph. Make sure that the body of the report matches the outline made for the paper.

Name: _____ Date: _____

Step 10: Writing the First Draft *(cont.)*

Conclusion

The conclusion summarizes the material that has been shared with the reader and offers a conclusion or insight about the thesis statement. It does not repeat the thesis statement!

How to write a conclusion without repeating the thesis statement:

- Restate the main idea in new words.
- Add a comment that shows the importance of the subject or an insight about it.
- Round out the report by referring to an idea in the introduction.
- Avoid introducing a new, unrelated idea.
- Avoid such phrases as "Now you have seen . . ." or "I have just told you about . . ."

Name: _____ Date: _____

Step 11: Revising and Writing the Final Draft

Ask yourself these questions:

1. Does my thesis statement (or thesis question) accurately reflect the content and the point of the report?

2. Have all points been covered in the paper?

3. Do details or facts support all of the main ideas?

4. Do I have unrelated information anywhere in the paper?

5. Do I have transitional sentences between paragraphs?

6. Does each paragraph have a topic sentence that relates to the thesis?

7. Is each idea supported by evidence from the research?

8. Have I checked for spelling and grammatical errors?

9. Have I had someone other than myself read the report?

Name: _____ Date: _____

Step 12: Works Cited Page

▮▮

This is the last step! You have now come to the end of the research paper. The works cited page is the list of materials used. If you have done the job correctly, you should have several source cards with citations on them. All you need to do for this last step is to alphabetize the source cards and write the citations on the works cited page. Be sure to use the correct heading. Follow the directions below, and check the form used on the sample works cited page that follows.

The information on the works cited page comes directly from the citations that are on your source cards. Only sources that have been used in parenthetical footnotes should be listed on the works cited page.

▮▮

Procedures

1. Arrange the entries in alphabetical order by the first word of the citation. A source with no author named is alphabetized by the first word of the title, not counting *A, An,* and *The.*

2. Begin the first line of each entry at the left margin, and indent succeeding lines of each entry five spaces from the left margin.

3. Space twice after the period that follows the author's name.

4. Space twice after the quotation marks following an article title from a periodical and twice after the period following a book title.

5. Space only once after other items of information, such as the colon that follows the city of publication, after commas, and between other information items.

Name: _____ Date: _____

Step 12: Works Cited Page *(cont.)*

Sample Works Cited Page

Works Cited

Brown, Ann Cole and Herbert Hobber. <u>Houghton-Mifflin English</u>. Boston: Houghton-Mifflin Co., 1990: 328–61.

Brown, Barbara. <u>Grammar and Composition</u>. 5th ed. Boston: Prentice Hall, 1984: 486.

Warriner, John E. <u>English is Funny!</u> Benchmark Edition. Orlando: Harcourt, Brace, Jovanovich, 1988: 232–236.

- Notice how the second line of each citation is indented five spaces.

- Remember to double-space between citation entries.

- Don't forget to alphabetize!

Chapter 9: Research Investigations

Overview

Often, a classroom teacher would like to set up a collaborative group research project that is integrated with the curriculum and uses the Web. Carolyn Hinshaw, of Bellingham Public Schools, has created an informational Web space that takes the classroom teacher through this process and also provides resources to support the research model. This information is found on the LearningSpace site on the Internet at *http://www.learningspace.org/instruct/lplan/rlesson.htm*.

Building the Research Problem or Question

Qualities of a research question or problem:

- Revolves around a unit of study.
- Is not easily solved or answered.
- Takes more than one person to solve.
- Pushes students to higher levels of thinking.
- Produces an answer or solution in the end by way of a written product.
- Involves a choice and asks students to invent answers or to create something new.

How to build a question or problem:

- **Be creative.** Coming up with an innovative, motivating, and interesting problem to solve is the hardest step. Oftentimes, placing the problem within a scenario description works best. Put the students in a setting, give them a role—such as a scientist—and pose a problem that needs to be solved.
- **Select a question that has many possible answers.** A simple question, such as "Which is the safest way to travel to school?" is sometimes the hardest one to answer.
- **Limit the possibilities.** Sometimes, especially with younger students or the first time through the investigation, helping students limit the possibilities is helpful and timesaving. An example would be: "Out of the following three explorers—Columbus, Magellan, and Cook—which of their discoveries had the most impact on future explorations of our world?"

Getting Organized

There are several questions a teacher needs to ask when creating research teams.

- How many students will be in research teams?
- How will the groups be determined?
- Which teamwork skills will be taught or stressed during the research?

Getting Organized *(cont.)*

When students meet to organize their teams, they need to ask a series of questions.

- Who will have which responsibilities?
- What is our plan on how we will work together?
- What resources will we use?
- How will we collect and organize our facts?
- What questions will we ask as we collect facts?

Gathering Information

During the information-gathering process, the teacher spends time teaching lessons on how to get information gathered and strategies to help groups accomplish their work. The teacher will also meet with teams to help them use the following strategies to find information they need.

Scan what you need to read. Look it over and ask yourself:

- What is the selection about?
- Does it look like this source will give me the information I need?

As you read, ask your research questions:

- What facts am I looking for?
- Do these facts help to answer the question?

As you gather facts, make sure to:

- Gather facts you understand.
- Use a few words, not a whole sentence.
- Spell words correctly.
- Make facts readable.
- Organize facts as you gather them, using a table or chart.

Sorting and Analyzing

In this step, the teacher needs to determine the way in which the students will sort and analyze information. Students will need to collect notes in some sort of organized fashion. Teachers need to teach students how to use criteria to rate information in order to select facts that will help support their final answers. This helps students to narrow which pieces of information will be helpful in supporting their final answers or solutions. When finished collecting information, the students will need to sort their facts by using the questions that follow.

Analyzing Questions for Students

- Do we have enough information?
- Do the facts we have help solve the problem or answer the question?
- Do we need to get more facts?
- Are all the facts accurate, and do the facts make sense?
- Which facts are critical for helping to make a decision?
- What is the criteria we will use to analyze the facts?

Creating the Final Answer or Solving the Problem

This is the synthesis stage. Students take what they now know and create something new. It is like trying to put a jigsaw puzzle together. The students take all the bits and pieces of information, and by asking questions, reorganizing the facts, and through discussions with their teams, the answers or solutions begin to appear. This is a creative time, but teams need to remember to base their answers and solutions on the information they have gathered and analyzed.

Analyzing Questions for Teams

Teams are now ready to take the analyzed information, and ask the following questions:

- How can we use the ideas and information gathered to create the new answer or solution?
- How will that final product look?
- What is the criteria for the final product?
- Who will do what to help create the final product?

Teacher Rubric for Design of Research Lessons

As you design your research investigation lesson, use the rubric below to help you keep the criteria involved in a quality research lesson in mind.

Rubric for Research Lessons

	Problem or Question	Gathering	Sorting	Analyzing	Final Product
4	Students, within a curricular area, generate questions and or problems around a topic.	Information is gathered from multiple electronic and non-electronic sources and cited properly.	Students develop computer based structure for sorting information. ie: database	Students have analyzed the information and have drawn their own conclusions.	Students effectively use a combination of media to communicate their findings through multiple senses and publish on the WWW.
3	Students, when given a topic, generate questions and or problems.	Information is gathered from multiple electronic and non-electronic sources.	Students and teacher brainstorm ideas for computer based sorting structures. Students develop sorting structure from the list.	Students analyze the information and with teacher guidance draw their own conclusions.	Students effectively use a combination of media to communicate their findings through multiple senses.
2	Students, with teacher help, generate questions and or problems.	Information is gathered from limited electronic and non-electronic sources.	Students, together with teacher, develop computer based sorting structure.	Students, with teacher guidance, analyze information and draw conclusions.	Students use a combination of media to communicate their findings.
1	Questions and or problems are teacher generated.	Information is gathered from non-electronic sources only.	Students use teacher generated computer based sorting structure.	Students restate information that has been gathered. ie: restating the facts only	Students use limited media to communicate their findings. ie: written report

Appendix: Items on CD-ROM

All of the worksheets are in Adobe Acrobat format (PDF). If you do not have the free Adobe Acrobat Reader, visit http://www.adobe.com/ to download it.

Chapter 2: Choosing a Topic

What I Know, Think I Know, Want to Know

Unlocking the Keywords

General Information

Fun and Games

Roadmap for Research: Completed

Roadmap for Research

Chapter 3: Documenting Information

Menu for Success Worksheet

Menu for Success

Home (Data) Base

Database Entry Information Sheet

Microsoft Access Database

Macintosh Text Database

Windows Text Database

Standard DBF Database

Microsoft Excel Spreadsheet

Filemaker Pro (3/4) Database

Microsoft Works Database

Chapter 4: Collecting Information

Oodles of Outlines: Keyword

Oodles of Outlines: Topic

Oodles of Outlines: Sentence

Questions to Myself

Questions to Myself Checklist

Chapter 5: Searching for Information

The Internet Card Catalog

Search Engines and Mr. Boole

How Does a Directory Work?

How Does a Search Engine Work?

Appendix: Items on CD-ROM *(cont.)*

Chapter 6: Evaluating the Information

You Be the Judge!

Critical Evaluation of a Web Site: Elementary School Level

Critical Evaluation of a Web Site: Middle School Level

Critical Evaluation of a Web Site: Advanced Level

5 W's Information Sheet for Evaluating Web Sites

5 W's of Evaluation (PDF)

5 W's of Evaluation (PowerPoint 2000)

Chapter 7: Using the People on the Internet

News for All

Chapter 8: Information Retrieval Skills System

Step 1:	Topic Selection
Step 2:	Search Strategy (SS1)
Step 2:	Search Strategy (SS2)
Step 2:	Search Strategy (Internet)
Steps 3 and 4:	Focusing the Topic and Preliminary Outlining
Step 5:	Thesis Statements (or Thesis Questions)
Step 6:	Source Cards
Step 7:	Note Cards
Step 8:	Sentence Outline
Step 8:	Sentence Outline
Step 10:	Writing the First Draft
Step 11:	Writing the Final Draft
Step 12:	Works Cited Page